AN AMERICAN TRAGEDY

Opera in Two Acts

Music by
Tobias Picker

Libretto by
Gene Scheer

based on the novel by Theodore Dreiser

Commissioned by The Metropolitan Opera

SCHOTT

www.schott-music.com

Mainz · London · Madrid · New York · Paris · Tokyo · Toronto

LICENSE NOTICE

CONTENTS

CHARACTERS

Clyde Griffiths	Baritone
Elvira Griffiths	Mezzo-Soprano
Young Clyde	Boy Soprano
5 Children	
Samuel Griffiths	Tenor
Elizabeth Griffiths	Mezzo-Soprano
Bella Griffiths	Soprano
Gilbert Griffiths	Tenor
Sondra Finchley	Mezzo-Soprano
Grace Marr	Soprano
Roberta Alden	Soprano
Orville Mason	Bass
Reverend McMillan	Tenor
Hortense	Soprano

Chorus

PREMIERE
2 December 2005, The Metropolitan Opera

Conductor: James Conlon
Production: Francesca Zambello
Set Design: Adrianne Lobel
Costume Design: Dunya Ramicova
Lighting Design: James F. Ingalls
Choreography: Doug Varone

Principal Roles:
Roberta Alden: Patricia Racette (soprano)
Sondra Finchley: Susan Graham (mezzo-soprano)
Clyde Griffiths: Nathan Gunn (baritone)
Elvira Griffiths: Dolora Zajick (mezzo-soprano)
Elizabeth Griffiths: Jennifer Larmore (mezzo-soprano)
Samuel Griffiths: Kim Begley (tenor)
Gilbert Griffiths: William Burden (tenor)
Orville Mason: Richard Bernstein (baritone)
Hortense: Anna Christy (soprano)

LIBRETTIST NOTE

Writing a libretto based on Theodore Dreiser's classic novel *An American Tragedy* posed significant challenges as well as exciting possibilities. The novel explores central aspects of the American character through a powerful story of passion, desire and tragedy, perfect elements for an operatic treatment. It also features, however, a group of deeply flawed characters, all of whom struggle to resist the cultural currents which ultimately dictate the choices they make.

My central concern, in addition to imagining a 800 page novel in dramatic and operatic terms, was to find a way to evoke empathy for the characters while allowing them to retain their human flaws. As it turns out, music provided the solution. Music helps reveal the emotional truths of this story and enables us to identify, in a compelling new way, with the humanity of Dreiser's characters.

It should not be surprising, then, that working with Tobias Picker on this project has been the greatest thrill of my professional life. His passion for the piece is limitless, and his profound talent an inspiration. I am similarly grateful for the wise counsel and friendship of director Francesca Zambello.

I also sought guidance from Theodore Dreiser himself. While writing the piece, I kept on my desk a copy of a March 13, 1931 letter that Dreiser sent to Jesse Lasky at Paramount Pictures, in which he bitterly complained about director Josef von Sternberg's 1931 film adaptation of *An American Tragedy.* Dreiser wrote:

> Sternberg and writer Samuel Hoffenstein have botched my novel. Their greatest fault has been in the characterizations. They have made Clyde an unsympathetic smart aleck who cares for only one thing, a girl, any kind of girl.... Clyde is a creature of circumstances, not a scheming, sex starved, drug store cowboy. There is no relentless pursuit, no inescapable web that compels this boy to act as he does.

> In addition to that, they have made of Clyde's love affair with Roberta a sordid thing. As they picture it, there is nothing idyllic about it, and there should be ... there must be....

> The whole thing can be summed up by saying that *An American Tragedy* is a progressive drama.... A certain chain of events leads to certain conclusions.

Were Dreiser alive to see this opera, I'd like to think that he would recognize his "inescapable web," his "progressive drama." And I suspect that he might enjoy hearing his creations reveal their souls through music.

— Gene Scheer

SYNOPSIS

ACT I

SCENE ONE: Late 1890s. On a street corner near a mission in the American Midwest, Elvira Griffiths, a missionary, leads her son Clyde and his siblings in a hymn. *('Tis so sweet to trust in Jesus - music by William J. Kirkpatrick and words by Louisa M.R. Stead)* Many years later, in a smart Chicago hotel, the adult Clyde, now a bell boy, flirts with the chambermaid Hortense. She rebuffs him, then delivers the news that his rich uncle, Samuel, a factory owner from New York, is staying at the hotel. In the hotel ballroom, business associates toast Samuel's success. *(Vanderbilt, Astor, Dupont, James J. Hill)* When the party breaks up, Clyde introduces himself, and Samuel offers him a job at his shirt factory in Lycurgus, New York. *(I own a factory)* When Hortense returns to make a date with him, Clyde tells her he has other plans.

SCENE TWO: At the shirt factory, Clyde, newly promoted to supervisor, learns the ropes from Samuel's son, Gilbert, who advises him to keep his hands off the ladies. *(You've got to keep the line moving)* At the closing bell, Clyde's eye is caught by Roberta, one of the workers, who arranges a rendezvous with a friend loudly enough for him to overhear. As Gilbert drives away, Clyde watches enviously, reflecting on his disappointments past and his hopes for the future. *(A motor car! There he goes!)*

SCENE THREE: In front of the music hall, Clyde chats up Roberta, telling her of his missionary background and recalling his mother's lectures on temptation, until her friend arrives. *(My mother runs a mission)* Later that evening, Roberta encounters Clyde by the riverbank. When she describes the magician. *(I mostly liked the magic)* at the music hall, Clyde wishes he had the magic power to make her dreams come true. They arrange to meet again the following night.

SCENE FOUR: Elizabeth Griffiths, Samuel's wife, chastises him *(You've done more than enough)* for taking a chance on his inexperienced nephew. Their daughter, Bella, arrives with her friend Sondra, newly returned from New York City. When Samuel announces that Clyde is coming to lunch, Gilbert sneers at his father's "discovery," piquing Sondra's interest. After the others exit, Sondra tells Bella how New York has changed her. *(New York has changed me)* Entering unseen, Clyde is captivated. When Samuel returns to introduce his nephew, Elizabeth is condescending, but Sondra flirts with him, confiding to Bella that she thinks he would make "a nice project."

SCENE FIVE: In front of Roberta's apartment, Clyde presses her to let him come in. *(Come on, Roberta)* Inside, she describes the place *(It's the farmhouse)* where she grew up, and Clyde dances with her. That night, on the Griffiths' patio, Gilbert flirts arrogantly with Sondra. When he leaves, she and Bella plot to invite Clyde to Bella's birthday party. As Sondra starts to compose an invitation, *(I've been thinking of you)* the scene shifts back to the apartment, where Roberta pours out her feelings to Clyde. *(Oh Clyde, you stir my deepest memories)* He slowly leads her to the bed.

Scene Six: At Bella's birthday party, Clyde dances with Sondra, as Gilbert, drunk and sarcastic, disparages his cousin to a group of friends. *(My cousin Clyde is from Chicago)* Sondra leads Clyde outside. When he describes his bellboy days, *(I wish I'd bought two of these)* she senses the power of his dreams. She suggests that he visit her at her parents' summerhouse. *(We have a cottage on a lake)* He kisses her passionately, then takes her back to the party and rushes out.

Scene Seven: Late that night, Clyde makes excuses *(It's a dizzy thing this society biz!)* for keeping Roberta waiting, but she cuts him short. When he asks what is wrong, she tells him she is pregnant. At first, he balks at her demand that they marry, saying he's just getting started in life, but when she burst into tears, *(You have to marry me, Clyde)* he gives her his promise, sending her home to her parents to wait until he has saved enough money to come for her.

ACT II

Scene One: On the front porch of her parents' house, Roberta reads through some letters *(Today I pretended)* she has written to Clyde, begging him to come soon. Meanwhile, dallying by a lake at Sondra's summerhouse, Clyde and Sondra declare their love. He exhorts her to run away with him, but she counsels patience. As the two revel in their dream of *(I feel like I've been waiting)* romance, Roberta senses that hers is shattered and closes a last letter with an ultimatum, threatening to reveal her secret if Clyde does not keep his promise. *(Dear Clyde, Unless I hear from you)*

Scene Two: At church in Lycurgus, after the sermon is completed, the congregation sings a communion hymn. *(Lord, King of Kings)* Clyde sits with Sondra's family. Roberta approaches Sondra at the close of the service; when she is momentarily distracted, Clyde draws Roberta apart and implores her not to expose him. *(It's not what you think)* Assuring her that his attentions to Sondra are all about furthering his career, he promises to meet Roberta at the Utica Station that night. Rejoining Sondra, Clyde tells her he will be busy at the factory for several days. Alone, he hatches a scheme to murder Roberta. *(It will not take too long)*

Scene Three: Boating on a lake, Clyde tells Roberta they will be married in the morning. She describes her feelings about their future and comments on the beauty of the lake. *(Isn't it still and peaceful?)* When she leans over the side, he raises his paddle but cannot bring himself to strike. Roberta tries to embrace him, but he swings his arms up to stop her, inadvertently knocking her off the boat. Ignoring her cries for help, he watches her drown.

Scene Four: The following Saturday, at the Griffiths' summer house, Samuel tells Clyde he is proud of him, saying Sondra is "quite a catch." Orville Mason, the district attorney, interrupts, asking Samuel to leave him alone with Clyde. Roberta's letters have been found in Clyde's trunk, and the sheriff is waiting to arrest him. Clyde protests that he has done nothing wrong, as Mason leads him away.

SCENE FIVE: At the Griffiths' home in Lycurgus, Elizabeth tactlessly bemoans Sondra's ruined reputation. *(Accused of murder!)* Bella and Gilbert urge their friend to forget Clyde and get on with her life, while the chorus is heard reading Roberta's letters in the newspaper. Elvira arrives and asks to see Samuel in private. She begs him to come to the courthouse and show his faith in Clyde. *(I believe my son)* Samuel replies that in paying for his nephew's defense, he has done all he can.

SCENE SIX: In Clyde's jail cell, Elvira visits her son, who continues to protest his innocence. Elvira compares his sufferings with Christ's, saying he must bear his cross, but adds that if he tells the truth about his change of heart, the jury will understand. *(You did nothing to deserve this)*

SCENE SEVEN: In the courtroom, Mason questions Clyde about his relations with Sondra and Roberta. Clyde describes the elopement, claiming it was Roberta's idea and insisting that he tried to save her. *(That was her plan, not mine)* When Mason confronts him with evidence that he planned the trip himself, the spectators cry out for justice. As the prosecution rests its case, *(You picked up that brochure)* Elvira prays, but the jury, unmoved, renders its verdict: guilty as charged.

SCENE EIGHT: In his cell, Clyde, awaiting execution, hears Sondra's voice reading her parting letter; *(Clyde, This letter is so that you will not think that someone once dear to you)* though she will never understand what he has done, she wishes him freedom and happiness. When Elvira comes to pray with him, he confesses at last that he could have saved Roberta. Elvira, weeping, reminds him that the mercy of God is equal to every sin. As he approaches the electric chair, *(Lord Jesus give me peace/'Tis so sweet to trust in Jesus)* his youthful self sings an old childhood hymn while Clyde prays for peace, for the strength to confront death.

AN AMERICAN TRAGEDY

ACT I

SCENE ONE

(Late 1890s. A street corner near a mission in a Midwestern city. We hear Young Clyde's voice through the darkness as the lights gradually come up on dusk—of a summer night.)

YOUNG CLYDE

'Tis so sweet to trust in Jesus,
and to take him at his word;
just to rest upon his promise,
and to know, "Thus saith the Lord."

Jesus, Jesus, how I trust him!
How I've proved him o'er and o'er!
Jesus, Jesus, precious Jesus!
O for grace to trust him more!

(The lights slowly come up on Elvira and her poorly clothed children. They are on a street corner proselytizing to a group of homeward bound individuals of diverse grades and walks of life. The group on the street is mostly indifferent to the religious pleas of Elvira and her children.)

ELVIRA AND CLYDE

O how sweet to trust in Jesus,
just to trust his cleansing blood;
and in simple faith to plunge me
'neath the healing, cleansing flood!

THE OTHER CHILDREN JOIN IN

Jesus, Jesus, how I trust him!
How I've proved him o'er and o'er!
Jesus, Jesus, precious Jesus!
O for grace to trust him more!

I'm so glad I learned to trust thee,
precious Jesus, Savior, friend;
and I know that thou art with me,
wilt be with me to the end.

Jesus, Jesus, how I trust him!
How I've proved him o'er and o'er!
Jesus, Jesus, precious Jesus!
O for grace to trust him more!

ELVIRA

    Clyde, go light the candles in the window.
    There are some matches in the Mission Hall.

CHILDREN

    I'm so glad I learned to trust thee,
    precious Jesus, Savior, friend;
    and I know that thou art with me,
    wilt be with me to the end.

(Young Clyde surreptitiously takes a gold lighter out of his pocket and uses it to light the candles.)

ELVIRA

    Christ walks with you every day and hour,
    by light and by dark, at dawn and at dusk.
    He will bind up our wounds and make us whole!

CHILDREN

    Jesus, Jesus, how I trust him!
    How I've proved him o'er and o'er!
    Jesus, Jesus, precious Jesus!
    O for grace to trust him more!
    And I know that thou art with me,
    wilt be with me to the end.

(Elvira and her children pack up their things and go back to the mission.)

(Present day (pre-World War I). On another part of the stage the lights come up on Clyde, who is wearing an expensive, beautifully tailored cashmere coat. He is in a luxurious suite in one of the best hotels in Chicago. He examines a walking stick and an expensive pocket watch and then, when he walks by a full-length mirror, admires his good looks. He takes a gold cigarette lighter out of his pocket and lights a cigarette. It is the same lighter that young Clyde used to light the candles. Hortense, an attractive chambermaid, comes into the hotel suite and observes him posturing in front of the mirror as a rich hotel guest.)

HORTENSE

    Would you look at J.P. Morgan!
    You look like those gents downstairs,
    congratulating each other on some business deal.

CLYDE

    No one will find out!

(Clyde quickly removes the cashmere coat, revealing his bellboy uniform.)

Hortense, go dancing with me tonight.
I bet you came up here just so I'd ask you.

HORTENSE

I don't chase men. They chase me.
Look at this!

(She becomes distracted when she sees a guest's mink stole that has been tossed over a chair. She drapes it across her shoulders and admires herself in the mirror.)

HORTENSE

So, Mr. Morgan...
(She models the coat for Clyde.)
What do you think?
How about buying me this little mink?
I'm sure it would be nothing at all,
nothing at all, nothing at all for a man rich as you.
For a generous gent all the favors I'd do.
I'd be ever so grateful,
ever so true.

CLYDE

Go with me to The Wigwam. Let's go tonight.

HORTENSE

Oh, Clyde, you're talking about a rag joint.
I'm talking 'bout mink.

CLYDE

Please come.
And wear your little black hat
and your red dress.

HORTENSE

(Aside) I'd rather wear this.

CLYDE

You look so cute in that.

HORTENSE

(Aside) I'd look better in this.

CLYDE

You know I'm crazy 'bout you.
Honest, I am. Can't you see?
I can't stop thinking 'bout you.
Dance with me.

(He begins to dance with her.)

They have a great band.
The music they play
makes you forget what preachers say.
Come with me.
Wear the black hat, the red dress!
I'll be worth it, I promise, I promise.
Come on, Hortense, please say yes!

HORTENSE

I'll think about it, Clyde Griffiths.

(She hands him the mink.)

Take it or I'll never be able to part with it.

(Clyde puts the mink away.)

CLYDE

Please, please just say yes.

HORTENSE

Clyde Griffiths!
You are so naïve.
A girl has only so much time.
I can't play with poor boys forever.
Others have asked, you know.

CLYDE

Don't mess with that Squires.
He's too old for you.

HORTENSE

Mister Squires!
I almost forgot!
He sent me here to tell you.
A Mister Samuel Griffiths just checked in this morning.
Squires says he is your uncle from New York.

CLYDE

> My uncle? My uncle?

HORTENSE

> Yes.
> That's why I'm here.
> I came up to tell you.

CLYDE

> My uncle?
> I've never even met him.
> But I used him as a reference when Squires hired me.
> He owns some sort of factory.
> That's what my mother told me.

HORTENSE

> Better go down and meet him.

CLYDE

> Don't forget about tonight.

(She exits. Clyde puts the coat back where he found it. He walks from his position in the hotel suite directly into the ballroom and watches his uncle enjoying after-dinner drinks with business associates. Clyde is in awe of his uncle's commanding presence.)

CHORUS

> Vanderbilt, Astor, Dupont, James J. Hill,
> J.B. Duke, Frick, Mellon, J.P. Morgan,
> Harriman, Carnegie, O.H. Payne,
> and now our friend, Sam Griffiths!

(All, including Samuel, laugh.)

SAMUEL

> Well not quite gentlemen.
> But I've got three hundred working for me.
> Three hundred! That's right, gentlemen.
> Here's to industry!
>
> Now my shirts will make you richer
> in all your stores throughout Chicago.
> Here's to industry!

CHORUS

> Now your shirts will make us richer
> in all our stores throughout Chicago.
> Here's to industry!
> The best shirts and collars made in America!

SAMUEL

> Three hundred sets of hands.
> Three hundred cutting, stamping, sewing, shrinking fabric,
> packing shirts and collars to send to cities
> all over this great country.
> Cities like Chicago!
> My shirts and collars!

CHORUS

> Here's to industry!
> Vanderbilt, Astor, Dupont, James J. Hill,
> J.B. Duke, Frick, Mellon, J.P. Morgan,
> Harriman, Carnegie, O.H. Payne,
> and now our friend, Sam Griffiths!

SAMUEL

> Well not quite, gentlemen.
> But who knows where hard work and hope will take you.
> I remember when I first started out
> in a factory not much bigger than my hotel suite.
> And now my new place, opened not two years ago,
> is three stories high, made of a new magical material:
> Concrete blocks! Concrete blocks!
> Beautiful stuff— can't burn.
> You just stack 'em high and long—
> more beautiful than gold bars.
> In no time—thirty thousand square feet producing the best
> shirts and collars made in America.

CHORUS

> Mister Samuel Griffiths of Lycurgus, New York!
> The best shirts and collars made in America!
> Three hundred employees working for you today.
> The best shirts and collars made in America!

SAMUEL

> Concrete blocks. Concrete blocks!

(Samuel raises his glass in a toast.)

To honor this great country, there's a promise we must keep—
With God's help let us work each day,
so the harvests that we reap
will one day be as bountiful as those in heaven.
To our companies, to our future,
to the country that we love.

CHORUS

To honor this great country, there's a promise we must keep—
With God's help let us work each day,
so the harvests that we reap
will one day be as bountiful as those in heaven.
To our companies, to our future,
to the country that we love.

SAMUEL

To the country that we love.

(As the toast concludes, Samuel walks downstage onto the terrace of the hotel. He takes a cigar out of his pocket. Clyde follows his uncle onto the terrace. Samuel looks but can't find matches or a lighter. Clyde pulls a gold lighter out of his pocket and gives it to him. Slowly, Samuel recognizes it.)

CLYDE

My name's Clyde Griffiths.
My father, Asa Griffiths, was your brother, I believe.

SAMUEL

This was my father's.

CLYDE

My father gave it to me before he died.
It was our secret.
Mother would have made him sell it,
use the money for the mission.

SAMUEL

So you are Asa's son?
Well, I'll be damned.
Clyde ... Clyde Griffiths.
Well, I'll be damned.
You look like your grandfather.

CLYDE

>My father almost never spoke of him.

SAMUEL

>Well, hardly a day goes by when I don't think of him.
>He'd light cigars with this on the porch
>and talk about his faith.
>Not religion! Just hard work and hope.
>Those were his commandments.
>Well, I'll be damned. Asa's boy!
>You're different from him.
>You've left the mission life.

CLYDE

>It's all right, I guess,
>but not for me.
>I'm looking for a chance to do something,
>be something.

SAMUEL

>So, the tips are pretty good here? *(Samuel smiles.)*

CLYDE

>Not too bad, but I can do a whole lot more
>than carry bags— A whole lot more.

SAMUEL

>I own a factory in a little town called Lycurgus.
>You could come and work for me.
>You'd do better than a bellhop.
>You'd start at the bottom, but with hard work and hope
>someday you might be someone in Lycurgus.
>Employee number three hundred and one!
>I must get back to those gentlemen there. *(He gestures to his colleagues.)*
>Think it over. I leave tomorrow.

(Clyde is stunned, speechless. Samuel smiles and moves to rejoin his colleagues.)

>*(To himself)*
>Clyde Griffiths! Asa's boy!
>Well, I'll be damned.
>Asa's boy! Well, I'll be damned.

(Throughout the scene above Hortense has been watching Clyde with his rich uncle. Clyde's new prospects have clearly caused her to rethink her reluctance to go dancing with Clyde that night. She flirtatiously comes over to Clyde.)

HORTENSE

So, Clydie Wydie,
I'll meet you at The Wigwam at nine.
They have a great band.
The music they play
will make us forget what preachers say.

CLYDE

You can't play with poor boys forever.
Go ask Squires.
As it turns out, I have plans.

SCENE TWO

(The Griffiths' shirt factory in Lycurgus, New York. Women are sitting at worktables, making shirts and stamping collars. It is about twenty minutes before five on a Friday night.)

ALL

Can't believe the heat in here.
Only March but it feels like July.
A few more, a few more to do,
A few more shirts and the week will be done.
The week always goes so slowly.
The weekend seems to fly right by.
Can't believe the heat in here.
Only March but it feels like July.

(Gilbert and Clyde enter.)

GILBERT

No mistakes. No mistakes.
You have to keep the line moving.
Get the collars to the stitchers on time.
Father says two months in the warehouse
is enough for a Griffiths.
Remember the family name must stand for reserve,
ability, energy and good judgment.

CLYDE

    I understand.

GILBERT

    I hope you do.
    Ladies, ladies,
    this is Mr. Clyde Griffiths, your new supervisor.
    He will report directly to me.

(Gilbert leads him to Roberta's table.)

    (To Clyde)
    There are still a few minutes left.

    (To Roberta)
    Show him, Roberta.
    They stamp one size then send it to the stitchers.

ROBERTA

    Mistakes happen if we're not careful.

CLYDE

    I see. I see.

GILBERT

    (Aside to Clyde)
    Your job is keeping the line moving.
    D'ya think you can manage that?
    Oh, and keep your hands off the ladies.

(The bell sounds. It is now 5 p.m. and the women get up from their work and go to pick up their things.)

GILBERT

    (With great self assurance)
    I'm going to a dinner party tonight.
    (Sarcastically)
    I'm sure you had quite a social calendar in Chicago.
    I'm afraid little Lycurgus can't compare.

(Roberta speaks loudly enough for Clyde to hear.)

ROBERTA

    Grace, how 'bout going to the music hall tonight?
    There's a magician all the way from San Francisco!

GRACE

    I would love to go.

ROBERTA

    Let's meet at eight. Don't be late. You're always late!

(She repeats the information to be certain that Clyde will overhear.)

    Let's meet at eight at the "Empire" under the marquee.

GRACE

    I'll be there.

ROBERTA

    … at eight.

(The women have all exited, and Gilbert continues from the window.)

ROBERTA

    This is something you won't want to miss.
    Can you believe it? All the way from California.
    I'll see you there.

GILBERT

    You look bewildered.

CLYDE

    … Just excited.

GILBERT

    (Sarcastically)
    I'm so happy for you.

CLYDE

    I thought now I'd find a nicer place to live.

GILBERT

    Father's paying you fifteen bucks a week!
    That should settle you in style.
    Look over by the church.
    I'm sure that would suit you well.

(Gilbert exits. Clyde watches as Gilbert gets into his car and drives away.)

CLYDE

A motorcar. There he goes.
What a car! What a car! What a beautiful car.
Burgundy red with wooden trim.
What would it feel like being him?
Driving to dinner to dance with friends.
The car twists like a smile as the road bends.
Arriving.
There I go!
The hum of the engine still in my veins.
A hum that sings what I've always known—
my future as bright as polished chrome.

I remember singing on the street.
Feeling the scorn of passersby.
Feeling I'd never get out, never get to try.
Hymns and prayers, hymns and prayers,
Nothing but disdainful stares.

But look at me now!
Fifteen a week and running this floor!
Hard work and hope.
A few years from now,
I can see it: more!

That pretty girl, what was her name?
I believe, I believe … yes, Roberta, that's right.
When she spoke to her friend she looked at me.

"The Empire at eight, under the marquee!"
I'm driving to dinner to dance with friends.
The car twists like a smile as the road bends.
Oh, to sit behind the wheel and feel nothing but ease
as I climb each hill.
Gravity can't hold me still.
To own a motorcar!
That motorcar!
Burgundy red with wooden trim.

SCENE THREE

(Roberta is waiting under the marquee of the Empire Vaudeville Theater. She is waiting for Grace and wonders if Clyde picked up on her hint at the factory and will show up at the theater. She paces back and forth and then buys a ticket. Clyde enters.)

CLYDE

    Good evening.

ROBERTA

    (Feigning surprise) Oh, good evening, Mr. Griffiths.

CLYDE

    I had not seen you before today.
    But I'm new here. And I've hardly left the warehouse.

ROBERTA

    I'm new here, too. I came six months ago.

CLYDE

    Where are you from?

ROBERTA

    A farm near Utica.

CLYDE

    I've mostly lived in cities.

ROBERTA

    There aren't any theaters where I'm from.
    Just a church …

CLYDE

    … I know about that.
    My mother runs a mission.
    When I was young she would stand on the street corners—
    sing hymns and preach about the evils of things like vaudeville.

    "I'm so glad I learned to trust thee,
    Precious Jesus, Savior, friend;
    and I know that thou art with me …

ROBERTA

    … wilt be with me to the end."

(While the scene continues with Roberta and Clyde, we see Elvira in the background lecturing young Clyde.)

YOUNG CLYDE

    I'm so glad I learned to trust thee,
    Precious Jesus, savior, friend;
    And I know that thou art with me
    Wilt be with me to the end.

ELVIRA

    Know that the devil tempts and pursues
    all of us mortals and particularly a child like you.
    Oh, my child, you must be strong.
    You have such a long road before you.

    Be ever watchful and cling to the teachings of our Savior.
    Listen to the voice of the Lord,
    guiding our footsteps safely to a heaven more beautiful
    than we can dream.

    It's getting late. Go and put out the candles.
    Then to bed. Say your prayers.
    God listens to all those who
    live a righteous life.

(Elvira and Young Clyde exit.)

CLYDE

    I don't mean to keep you.

ROBERTA

    I am waiting for a friend.
    Are you coming?

(Clyde is disappointed when she mentions a friend.)

CLYDE

    No— thought I'd walk around a bit.
    I'm looking for a new place.

ROBERTA

    You're moving up fast.
    But you're a Griffiths.
    The best places are down by the river.
    It's nice. On weekends people swim and picnic there.

CLYDE

Do you?

ROBERTA

I never learned to swim, but I do love picnics.
Here she comes. *(Roberta sees Grace approach.)*

CLYDE

By the river you say?
(She nods.)
Nice to meet you, Miss…

ROBERTA

Alden … Roberta Alden.

(Grace and Roberta enter the theater. Clyde lights a cigarette with his gold lighter. From inside the theater we hear the orchestral accompaniment of a vaudeville show. The marquee pulls away, revealing Roberta. The space on the stage is now transformed to the park along the riverbank. It is a beautiful evening.)

CLYDE

Out for a walk?

ROBERTA

Just going home.

CLYDE

Where is your friend?

ROBERTA

Grace has gone home.

CLYDE

How was the show?

ROBERTA

I mostly liked the magic.
How he made the woman disappear.
He placed her on a swing,
waved his hand,
put a veil over her head,
pushed her higher and higher.
And then spoke
the magic words Aladdin said

ROBERTA (CON'T.)

>to make a wish come true:
>"Shazaar! Shazaar!"
>Then from his pocket he pulled out
>magic dust,
>threw it into the air!
>The veil fell to the floor.
>The woman wasn't there.

CLYDE

>I would like to do magic.
>But I'm out of magic dust.
>(*Looking through his pockets—trying to be charming.*)

ROBERTA

>No magic dust? Mr. Griffiths, you should not be so honest.
>You should let a woman think that you might …

CLYDE

(Finishing her thought.)

>…make her dreams come true.

ROBERTA

>Don't make fun.
>It was not a dream that led me here.
>My parents are poor; I moved for the job.

CLYDE

>Miss Alden, I'm glad you walked by here.
>You look very beautiful in the moonlight.

ROBERTA

>Oh, Mr. Griffiths, you're a dreadful flatterer.
>Next thing I know you are going to come over here
>and whisper …

CLYDE

>I don't think I ever saw a girl so pretty.

ROBERTA

>A dreadful, dangerous, wonderful flatterer.
>Yes … Well …
>Tell me, Mister Griffiths,
>Did you see the houses with the rooms to rent?

CLYDE

>Yes. I'll come by tomorrow.
>Is there anything I can do for you?
>Anything at all …

ROBERTA

>You're granting me a wish?
>I wish—to know why
>you would leave Chicago to come to Lycurgus?

CLYDE

>I'll tell you why tomorrow night.
>Meet me here tomorrow at six.
>No one will know.
>
>I wish to know you better, Miss Alden.
>Until tomorrow night.

ROBERTA

>I wish to know you better, Mister Griffiths.
>Good night, Mr. Griffiths—until tomorrow night.

(He takes her hand and gently kisses it.)

SCENE FOUR

(The patio off the back of the Griffiths' lavish home. There are French doors leading out onto the patio as well as large windows, which afford the audience a glimpse of the luxurious décor within the house. Clyde has been invited for lunch, but has not yet arrived. Samuel and Elizabeth Griffiths are seated outside.)

ELIZABETH

>You've done more than enough.
>I can't believe you took him on.
>No experience. No education.

SAMUEL

>He's my nephew.
>It's only lunch.

ELIZABETH

Well, a luncheon seems just right.
But let's not let it go on and on.
I must prepare for the party tonight.

I know what you're thinking.
If father had willed more of the money to Asa
his life might have been different.

It would have been wasted on
Salvation Army trombones.
You got thirty thousand.
You showed thirty times the promise.

It was his choice.
He told you not to tell Asa.
He knew it would be wasted on him.
You built your father's legacy.
It was his choice— not yours.

(Bella and Sondra enter.)

BELLA

Father! Mother!
Look who I found!
Back from New York City!
Just in time for the party tonight!

SAMUEL

Welcome back, Sondra.

ELIZABETH

You look wonderful.
Quite the lady.
Look what she's wearing.

SONDRA

I have another one for you. *(Referring to a hat)*
And a dress especially for the party.

(She hands Bella a gift box, which she opens.)

BELLA

A dress from a New York couturier!
It's just stunning!
You are too sweet.

SONDRA

> I bought gifts for all of you—
> in Gilbert's motorcar.

ELIZABETH

> *(Surprised)* Gilbert!

BELLA

> We picked her up at the station.
> *(Aside to mother)* I forced him.
> Now tell us about your trip.
> I want to hear everything.

(Gilbert enters.)

SAMUEL

> She will have to regale us later.
> My nephew Clyde is coming for lunch.

GILBERT

(With great sarcasm)

> Father's discovery!
> He works at the factory—some months now.
> He met him working at a hotel in Chicago.
> No experience. No education.
> You'd be bored by him.
> I am.

SONDRA

> *(To Gilbert)*
> I see. It is quite clear.
> He must be handsome.
> You must be jealous.
> You're jaded and bored, Gilbert Griffiths.
> You need to spend some time in New York City.
> The city would change the way you feel.

ELIZABETH

> Look how she talks.
> She has become quite a sophisticate.

SAMUEL

> Come, let's go in and wait for Clyde.

GILBERT

Yes. Let's …

SAMUEL

Lunch, Sondra?

SONDRA

No time … but I'll see you tonight.

SAMUEL

Say hello to your parents.

ELIZABETH

Bella?

BELLA

In a moment, Mother.

(Samuel, Bella and Gilbert exit. Bella is very excited. She wants to hear all the gossip about Sondra's trip.)

BELLA

So what was it like? Did you get any time alone?
Away from your father?

SONDRA

Yes, I hardly ever saw him.

BELLA

Tell me everything.

SONDRA

New York has changed me.
I just felt so alive there.
And now awakened and surprised,
I see the world through different eyes.

New York reaches out like the Brooklyn Bridge.
It begs you to feel its current,
to add your voice to the constant chorus.
You should see Fifth Avenue!
People wrapped in elegant clothes:
scarves from Persia, jewels from St. Petersburg,
perfume from Paris. All the world is in New York.

Look at this fabric.
I've never seen such colors.
The city's filled with treasures.
We must go back, explore each one.

*(Clyde, escorted by a servant, enters. The servant exits and, unobserved, Clyde watches
Sondra from the shadows.)*

New York is both crowded and vast,
blending contests and delights,
with energetic days, romantic nights.
Desire reaches everywhere,
like buildings rising through the air.

I went to the opera, was admired by men
watching me, not the stage.
As the heroine lay dying in her lover's arms,
every eye was filled with tears,
but those of one young man,
whose eyes were fixed on mine.
I never had a man around here
look at me like that before.

New York has changed me.
My heart has been released.
And now awakened and surprised,
I see the world through a lover's eyes.

New York has changed me.
New York would change anyone.

(Sondra mistakes Clyde for Gilbert.)

Sondra

Gilbert Griffiths! Always lurking in the shadows.

(Clyde steps forward.)

Clyde

I'm sorry. I did not mean to…

Sondra

Oh, forgive me. You looked like Gilbert.
But in the light I can see
Gilbert only wishes he looked like you.
You must be…

(Samuel, Elizabeth and Gilbert enter.)

SAMUEL

Clyde, there you are!

CLYDE

I came in the side. I thought it was the front.

ELIZABETH

Of course you did.

SAMUEL

Easy to get lost here.
Come here and meet your Aunt Elizabeth,
Bella. You know Gilbert.
And this is a friend of ours, Sondra Finchley.

CLYDE

It's very nice to meet you all.
Your description of New York was … mesmerizing

SONDRA

I understand you are from Chicago.

CLYDE

All over, really. My mother is now in Denver.
I worked out West, too ...

ELIZABETH

(Condescendingly)
Is your mother still doing religious work?

CLYDE

Yes.

ELIZABETH

Well, we look forward to hearing all about it.

GILBERT

Tennis starts at two!

SAMUEL

*(To Gilbert)*You could help Sondra with the packages.

GILBERT

> I will be late as it is.
> (*He exits.*)

CLYDE

> I'd be glad to help.

SAMUEL

> Well done, Clyde.
> We will wait for you inside.

ELIZABETH

> Come along.

BELLA

> I'll just try this on, mother.

ELIZABETH

> You have things to do before the party tonight.

> (*She is tactless—mentioning the party to which Clyde is not invited.*)

(*Bella, Elizabeth and Samuel exit into the house. Sondra and Clyde walk across stage to Gilbert's car.*)

SONDRA

> You worked in a hotel?
> I bet you were a bellhop.

CLYDE

> How'd you figure that?

SONDRA

> It can't be just your good looks
> why Gilbert doesn't like you.
> Oh, don't act so surprised!
> You must be a poor relation.
> I saw it in his eyes.
> No one likes to be reminded of who they'd be
> without their father's money.

CLYDE

> You are right about that.
> Still, I suppose he's harmless …

SONDRA

> … Oh, you poor thing. He is nothing of the kind.

CLYDE

> I've read your name in the papers.
> Horseback riding and tennis contests.
> I saw your picture, too.
> You looked like an angel in the flower parade.

SONDRA

> Do you flatter all the girls with such ease?

CLYDE

> There are no other girls.

SONDRA

> That's hard to imagine.

CLYDE

> What did you buy for yourself?

SONDRA

> This hat.
> Do you think I should have chosen lavender?

CLYDE

> It's perfect.

Bella enters wearing her new dress.

BELLA

> Sondra, I just love it.
> At the party we will be so fashionably dressed.
> *(To Clyde)* Lunch looks delicious.

(Clyde picks up the packages and walks towards the house.)

> *(To Clyde)*
> I want to hear *all* about you.

CLYDE

Nice to meet you, Miss Finchley.

BELLA

See you tonight.

SONDRA

Is Clyde coming, too?

BELLA

Mother won't hear of it.

(Clyde overhears that he is not invited. He registers the slight and then exits.)

SONDRA

I think he would make a nice project.

BELLA

I know you, Sondra.
You want to make my evil brother cross.
Sounds like fun.

SONDRA

Enjoy lunch.

BELLA

Don't be late.

SCENE FIVE

(In front of Roberta's apartment. On the other side of the stage, the back of the Griffiths' home is dimly lit but in view.)

CLYDE

Come on, Roberta. You know I'm crazy about you.
Honest I am.
It's been six weeks.
Let me come in for a while.
Six long weeks.
It's Saturday night.
You know how much I care for you by now.
I'll just stay for a while.

ROBERTA

>People would know.
>You know that.

CLYDE

>Trust me.

ROBERTA

>It wouldn't be right.
>Someone might see.

CLYDE

>No one's around.
>Why shouldn't we go in?
>Why?
>Others do it.

ROBERTA

>Well, maybe your cousin Gilbert's set.
>They probably put ideas into your head
>at lunch today.

CLYDE

>I'm getting tired of walking the streets every night,
>hiding all the time.

ROBERTA

>Oh please, Clyde, don't be mad.

(She kisses him. He moves to leave.)

ROBERTA

>Please don't go, Clyde.
>Please don't leave me.
>I love you so, Clyde.
>I would if I could. You know that.
>I love you so.
>You know I do.

CLYDE

>Oh, Bertie.

(They kiss and move into the apartment.)

ROBERTA

> Please … be very quiet.

CLYDE

> I like your place. Look at all these books.
> *(Clyde sees a photograph.)*
> What is this photograph?

ROBERTA

> It's the farm-house where I grew up
> with its broken porch steps.
> There's the swing on the maple tree,
> where I read and imagined—
> all the things I hoped I feel—
> All the things that brought me comfort,
> I feel again when I'm with you.
> Oh, Clyde, you stir my deepest memories.
> The slightest things, almost forgotten,
> still inside of me,
> silently shaping all I am.

CLYDE

> Miss Alden, would you dance with me?

ROBERTA

> *(Coyly)*
> Just a dance, Mr. Griffiths?

(On the other side of the stage the lights come back up on the patio of the Griffiths' home. The lights dim on Clyde and Roberta. They continue to dance slowly in the shadows. They stop to kiss and then continue their slow dance while the action continues on the other side of the stage. Gilbert and Sondra walk out the French doors onto the patio. It is after dinner. Gilbert is smoking a cigar.)

GILBERT

> Who should I take to Bella's birthday?
> It should be quite a party.

SONDRA

> Are you asking me?

(Gilbert ignores Sondra's question. He continues.)

GILBERT

I can't decide.
I thought you might help me.
Katherine's eyes are sparkling starlight.
Helen's skin—as flawless as pearls.
Oh Sondra, I'm sure you can tell me
which I should ask of these girls.

(Gilbert begins dancing by himself. He is full of himself. As he begins, Sondra continues. She knows quite well that talk of Clyde will irritate Gilbert.)

SONDRA

I enjoyed meeting your cousin Clyde.
I hear he's moving up fast.

(Bella comes out of the house onto the patio.)

GILBERT

Dance with me, B.

(Gilbert dances with his sister.)

BELLA

Doesn't he dance swell?

(Sondra rolls her eyes.)

Father wants you.
They are going into the library for cognac.

GILBERT

(Enthusiastically)
The cognac from Chicago.
Something good from Chicago.

(Gilbert exits into the house.)

SONDRA

Have the invitations gone out?
It would be such a lark …

BELLA

… if we invited Clyde.

BELLA AND SONDRA

Just to see how he would do.
You just want to see…

SONDRA AND BELLA

Gilbert's face when Clyde walks in!

BELLA

Terribly awful—terribly fun.
I saw a spark in his eye when you looked at him.
You'll write a note.
I'll enclose it with the invitation.
This is just perfect—terribly fun.
Think about something to say.
I'll get you pen and paper …

(Bella goes into the house. The lights come back up on Roberta and Clyde.)

ROBERTA

Clyde, you stir my deepest memories.
The slightest things, almost forgotten,
still inside of me,
silently shaping all I am.

I've been thinking of you, Clyde.
You know why.
I love you so.
Oh, to make you happy.
Let me try.
You won't be sorry if you hold—
Come hold me close.
Close as you want.
Clyde, I am so happy tonight in your arms.
Come over here.
Come let me make you happy.

(Bella returns and Sondra composes a note to Clyde.)

SONDRA

I have been thinking of you,
I don't know quite why.
I hope you will come to Bella's party.
I hope you will try.

SONDRA (CON'T.)

The others thought me silly
waxing poetic about a city.
Not you. Not you.

I have been thinking of you,
I don't know quite why.
I hope you will come.
You won't be sorry if you come play with us.
You'd make Bella happy if you'd come.
Clyde, I'd be happy too.

CLYDE

It's been six weeks now.
You know how much I care for you.
I've been thinking of you.
You know why.
Close your eyes.
Just forget everything.
You have changed me.
Oh, if you knew how I want you.

(By the end of the trio Clyde has taken Roberta into the bed.)

SCENE SIX

(As the stage gradually fills with people doing a popular dance, the set is transformed into a party scene celebrating Bella's birthday. Clyde, dressed in a dinner jacket, joins the group and dances with Sondra.)

(Gilbert is drunk, condescending. He is singing to a group of friends. Clyde and Sondra are focused on each other. They are oblivious to Gilbert's hostile tone.)

GILBERT

My cousin Clyde is from Chicago.
He was big in the hotel business.
I bet the bellhops told him
all of the best places to dance.
Look at him!

BELLA

Gilbert! You're drunk.

(The chorus gossips to each other.)

CHORUS

His cousin Clyde is from Chicago.
He was big in the hotel business.
You bet the bellhops told him
all of the best places to dance.
Look at him!

GILBERT

All the best new dances, the best music,
come from Chicago.

(Clyde, who has been dancing with Sondra, goes to get them drinks. Sondra becomes aware of Gilbert's sarcastic, mean-spirited behavior. She is embarrassed.)

He's from Chicago.
He must know William Thompson.
Of course he knows him!
He worked at his father's hotel!
He must love their place on Lake Michigan.
Father says that it's twice the size of our homes upstate.

SONDRA

Gin enhances your many charms.

GILBERT

Gin enhances my many charms.
My many charms are enhanced by gin!
I can see games being played by pretty rich girls.
Here's to pretty rich girls!

CHORUS

Gin enhances your charms!

(Gilbert rejoins his friends. Another dance begins. Sondra goes to Clyde, takes his hand, and leads him out of the club.)

SONDRA

Let's get out of here.

(Sondra and Clyde walk downstage. Some sort of movement and lighting allow Sondra and Clyde to leave the party. They are alone and continue the scene.)

CLYDE

When I worked at that hotel,
sometimes I'd try on a finely tailored coat
of some fancy guest.
I'd pick up his things—
hold them in my hands.
I'd imagine I was that guest—not me.

I felt dreams in their pockets.
I'd put my hands inside
and pull out the last thing they dreamt.
I once wore Carnegie's coat.

SONDRA

And what was the last thing he dreamt?

(Clyde pretends to be Andrew Carnegie.)

CLYDE

I wish I had bought two of these in Paris last winter.
This fabric is softer than the hands
of those French girls who pulled each stitch—
softer than their silken breath.

SONDRA

Mister Carnegie—
You've been everywhere.
How does our city compare?

CLYDE

Chicago is like a woman begging for attention—
But Paris is a woman, turning her head, forcing you to dream.
I wish ... I wish ... I'd bought two.

(Clyde puts his coat on Sondra's shoulders. As he does so, he touches her.)

SONDRA

Clyde Griffiths, you're quite a flirt.

CLYDE

The only reason I came tonight
is 'cause I knew I'd see you.
I've not thought of anything, anyone,
since I saw you last.

SONDRA

Are your dreams inside these pockets?

(She reaches into the pockets of the coat.)

CLYDE

You tell me.

(She takes her time, walks around, and plays the game of trying to imagine being Clyde.)

SONDRA

I feel … I feel … hopeful and powerful …
… and something not quite contained,
like water clinging to the brim of a cup.
One false move and …
(She takes his hand.)
… splash.

CLYDE

Are you really going to be away all summer?

SONDRA

We have a cottage on a lake in the mountains.
The breeze is scented with spruce.
Every summer we retreat away from city.
You must come and see.
It is the place I feel truly free.
Oh, Clyde, I'd like to show you this place
that means so much to me.
Riding and swimming, boating all day long.
It's a glorious time.
But my favorite thing is diving—
Twenty feet in the air—
I raise my arms, stand on my toes.
I reach and dive with my eyes closed.
I twist and reach and fall free
and wait for the water to catch me.
You must come and spend
some weekends together with me.
I'll twist and turn and fall free.
You be the lake and catch me.
Clyde, can you catch me?

(The party once again becomes visible to the audience. People are dancing, having a good time.)

CLYDE

Of course I will.
You are so beautiful. You know you are.
I think about you all the time.

SONDRA

I'm sure I ought not let you say those things to me.
Still, you are so sweet.
We have all the time in the world.

(The lights come up on Roberta. She is in her apartment waiting for Clyde. He is late and she is clearly distressed. Clyde takes his coat from Sondra and puts it back on.)

CLYDE

Hopeful and powerful and ... *(He kisses her passionately.)*

(He escorts her back to the party and quickly exits. Sondra rejoins her friends. She resumes dancing. The dance continues as Clyde goes to Roberta's apartment. The choreography leads all of the dancers off stage and Clyde is left alone outside of Roberta's apartment.)

SCENE SEVEN

(Roberta's apartment. It is after 11 p.m. She has been waiting for Clyde, who is over two hours late. She reads the society page from a window seat, puts down the paper, paces, and then returns to the window and looks for Clyde. Finally, she sees him approaching. She stands up, walks across the small apartment and opens the door for him. Clyde is nervous, and as he is taking off his jacket, begins anxiously making an excuse for being so late.)

CLYDE

It's a dizzy thing, this society biz!
I never saw a town like this before.
You do one thing with these people,
and they must do something more.

ROBERTA

Clyde Griffiths, how can you treat me like this?

CLYDE

Bertie, I know it's late.

ROBERTA

> I'm tired of hearing your excuses.
> Time after time.
> It doesn't matter anymore.

(Clyde is not listening to her. He is more concerned with making an excuse.)

CLYDE

> I thought dinner would begin at seven
> and end in time.
> But it didn't start 'til nine
> and broke up just a few minutes ago.
> Isn't that the limit? Can you believe …

ROBERTA

> Oh Clyde, stop!
> Not now. Oh, Clyde!

CLYDE

> What is it Bertie? Tell me what's wrong.
> You're trembling.
> I said I'm sorry— really I am.
> There was nothing I could do …

ROBERTA

> Clyde, you said if anything went wrong
> you'd help me.

CLYDE

> Of course, Bertie.

ROBERTA

> Something's wrong.

CLYDE

> Tell me, Bertie. What is wrong?

ROBERTA

> I hardly know how to tell you.
> Oh, Clyde. Oh, Clyde, I waited so I could be sure.
> I'm past my time.

CLYDE

> How can you be sure?

ROBERTA

It's true. Clyde, it's never been like this.

CLYDE

Who have you told?

ROBERTA

Not a soul.
I almost told you at the factory today.

CLYDE

Roberta!

ROBERTA

There's only one thing to do.
Marry me, Clyde.

CLYDE

Hold on. Hold on.
I don't see how I can.
All I have is my job.
The family doesn't know about you—
Not a thing … and should all this suddenly come out,
they are sure to fire me—cut me off.
What would I do?
It would go hard with both of us.

ROBERTA

You have to marry me, Clyde.
You cannot leave me now.
I waited for you at the window.
Praying you'd appear.

CLYDE

But marrying!
That would fix things for you.
What about me and all I'd planned?
I'm just getting started here.

ROBERTA

How can you be like this, Clyde?
I read the papers, the society page.
I've seen those pictures of over-privileged rich girls.
Is that it?
Is that it, Clyde?

CLYDE

>Those girls have nothing to do with this.
>Nothing!
>I want to do the right thing,
>but I'm just getting started.

ROBERTA

>I wish ... I wish I could dress like they do.
>They've got everything.
>You know they have.
>
>I don't want to keep your dreams from coming true.
>Stay with me, Clyde ...
>Oh, Clyde. I would do anything for you.

CLYDE

>*(Frustrated)* Roberta!

ROBERTA

>I'll even let you go off someday.
>But you must marry me!
>Just do what's right.

(She breaks down crying.)

CLYDE

>All right! All right! I will marry you then.
>It will soon be all right.
>I'll need some time to save some money.
>Surely you understand that.
>Go to your folks.
>Then very soon I'll come for you.

ROBERTA

>You promise?

CLYDE

>I promise.

CURTAIN ACT 1

ACT II

SCENE ONE

(The front porch of Roberta's parents' house. She is alone on stage and reads the letter she has just written to Clyde.)

ROBERTA

Today I pretended you'd be here soon.
So, I bid goodbye to all of my favorite places.
Those secret nooks, all the secret places that are so dear to me.
Places I have known almost all of my life.
The springhouse with its great masses of green moss.
The beehive, the house in the orchard.
Goodbye to the neighbors.
Those kind people who mended all my dresses
and saved me the thrashing that I deserved.
Mama's made me a fine new silken dress.
But every time it is fitted,
I break down. I'm so frightened.
I don't care where you go,
what you're doing, who you've been with.
Just come for me soon.
Don't leave me here.
I can't lie to poor dear Mama anymore.
Please think of all I had to give up.
The summer's pleasure has been lost
waiting for you.
My dear Clyde, I cannot wait forever.
Not forever.
You must come for me, take me away.
Heaven bless you.

(The lights fade on Roberta. The lights reveal Sondra and Clyde, who are seated on a dock. Their bare feet dangle in the lake. They are both dressed in summer attire.)

SONDRA

We should go dancing tonight.
I will wear the hat I wore the day we met.
Do you remember, Clyde?

CLYDE

I remember every detail.
The hat was yellow.
There was a dinner.
I wasn't invited.

SONDRA

Your uncle spoke to my father. *(Clyde looks at her for reassurance.)*
And now Father's coming round.
All it takes is time …
We have all the time in the world.

CLYDE

The lake is so beautiful.
Just like my Sondra.
If you only knew how much I love you.
If I could only tell you … tell you all … tell you everything.
How I wish I could let you know everything.

SONDRA

I know all I need to know.
I know you love me. I know I love you.
We will share our life together.
We'll stay together, you'll see.
Oh, Clyde, it does not matter what happens now.
You just wait and see.
I will never give you up.

I know next Sunday in Lycurgus,
You'll come to church with my family.
I have the most beautiful dress to wear.
You can join us in our family pew.
It will be so wonderful.

CLYDE

(With a great sense of urgency)
Sondra, run away with me now.
I want you so much.
I need you.
How I love you.
How I adore you.

SONDRA

Be patient. We have time.
So much time. Be patient, Clyde.
How many times have I written to you?
How many times have I whispered
I won't give you up?
I never loved before,
but I do love you, Clyde.
Slowly, they'll understand.

SONDRA (CON'T.)

    Something wonderful has happened.
They will see what I see in you—
how I adore you.

(Clyde looks distressed. Sondra flirtatiously picks up Clyde's jacket, which is lying on the dock. She puts it on as she did on the night of Bella's party.)

SONDRA

    What are you thinking, Clyde?

CLYDE

    Just this.

(Clyde kisses Sondra. While they are kissing, the lights come back up on Roberta.)

ROBERTA

    Clyde, I feel as though you are not coming.
Six long weeks have gone.
Six weeks have gone and you've hardly called.
Do you feel nothing at all?
You have promised to marry me
and I feel like I'm never going to see you again.
Are you coming?

SONDRA AND ROBERTA

    I feel like I've been waiting.
A whole life waiting to be desired by someone like you.
What we share will bind us both forever.
Just let me, I will make your dreams come true.
Oh, to feel you'll never be alone,
to know each day will start
with one who knows the secrets of your heart.

ROBERTA

    Clyde, you said you'd always love me.
I know you can find work in some small town.
The farms will soon need men for the harvest.
Our future will be wonderful, you'll see.
Come for me, Clyde. Come for me, Clyde.
You promised me. You promised me.
Don't leave me now.
Please, Clyde.

SONDRA

Clyde, we'll go to Paris, all the places you've dreamed of.
I won't leave you.
Our future will be wonderful, you'll see.
Come with me, Clyde. Come with me, Clyde.
I promise you. I promise you my heart.
Be patient, Clyde.
All that we want is waiting for us.

(Sondra and Clyde kiss and exit.)

ROBERTA

Dear Clyde,
Unless I hear from you
by telephone or letter before Friday noon,
I shall come to Lycurgus.
The world will know
how you have treated me.
My whole life is ruined.
Yours will be, too.
I cannot feel I'm entirely to blame.
I have done all I could
to make this burden
as easy for you as possible.
I certainly regret all the misery
it will cause my parents and friends
and all whom you know and hold dear.
But I will not wait;
I will not suffer one hour more.

SCENE TWO

(A church in Lycurgus. Sondra is seated next to Clyde and her family in one of the first pews.)

McMILLAN

And so Jesus said, "You will see a donkey
tied with its colt beside it.
Untie them, bring them here.
Just say the master needs them."
And so they fulfilled the ancient prophecy,
Tell Jerusalem her King is coming to her,
riding humbly on a donkey's colt.

McMILLAN (CON'T.)

And the disciples threw their garments
over the colt for Jesus to ride on.
And some in the crowd threw their coats
on the road ahead of him.
And they shouted:
"God Bless David's son.
God's Man is here.
Praise God in the highest heaven!"

(The congregation rises and walks down the aisle to the front of the church for Communion.)

CHORUS

Lord, King of Kings you are the way.
You are the truth that ends all strife.
You are the spirit that gives me breath.
You are the love that conquers death.

Praise the Father and the Son,
the Holy Spirit that makes all one.
To redeem our sins, His son he gave.
God's love alone transcends the grave.

(Roberta enters the back of the church. Clyde sees her. She notices that he is sitting next to Sondra Finchley.)

Blood of our savior, come, make me worthy.
Feast of the flesh, Come, sanctify my soul.
Let me become your hands here on earth.
Make of my death an eternal birth.

Praise the Father and the Son,
the Holy Spirit that makes all one.
To redeem our sins, His son he gave.
God's love alone transcends the grave.

Father in heaven, humbly I beseech thee.
May I know the joy of your embrace.
A quiet surrender, a quiet release.
A quiet unfolding to unending peace.

(Roberta is the last person to receive Communion. Clyde has already received Communion with Sondra and her family and has returned to one of the first pews.)

Praise the Father and the Son,
the Holy Spirit that makes all one.
To redeem our sins, His son he gave.
God's love alone transcends the grave.

McMillan

Go in peace.

(The congregation exits and Roberta approaches Sondra.)

Roberta

Miss Finchley?

Sondra

Yes.

Roberta

I work at the factory …

(Clyde glares at Roberta, appeals to her not to reveal the truth.)

Sondra

My father's factory?

Roberta

No …
I need … I need to ask …
I've seen many pictures of you
in the society page.
You always look so beautiful;
your clothes are always perfect.

Sondra

Thank you.
That is very kind of you to say.

(Sondra is momentarily distracted by a congregant who gestures to her to come over to speak to someone.)

Clyde
(Aside to Roberta)

No, Roberta.
Please, Roberta!
I love you. You don't understand.

(Roberta pauses and then decides to lie for Clyde one last time. Sondra returns.)

ROBERTA

> We're collecting old clothing for the poor.
> If you've anything to give,
> bring it to the church next week.

SONDRA

> Clyde, this woman
> is collecting old clothing for the poor.
> I'll see if I can part with anything.

(Sondra is called away again and this time exits the church, where a number of the congregants are chatting with each other. Roberta turns away. She moves to a discreet place in the church. She is on the verge of tears. Clyde approaches Roberta and quietly tries to explain the situation.)

CLYDE

> *(To Roberta)*
> It's not what you think!
> Her father owns a factory.
> You know … when we are married,
> I'll need a job.
> For you, for us, for the child.
> I think he wants to hire me …

ROBERTA

> No more waiting. No more lies.
> Tonight?
> You've promised me.
> I love you, Clyde.
> I was ready to reveal everything.
> But you see—I do love you.
> We will enjoy the last days of summer
> on our honeymoon.
> This is our chance …
> One last chance.
> I'll meet you there tonight.

CLYDE

> All right. Tonight.
> Meet me tonight.
> Meet me at the Utica Station.
> I'll do what I promised. I'll meet you tonight.
> Meet me at the Utica Station.
> I'll do what I promised.

I'll marry you. I'll do what's right.
I'll meet you tonight.

(Roberta exits. Clyde joins Sondra, who is waiting for him outside of the church. Most of the other congregants have exited. Clyde and Sondra walk away from those who remain. During the beginning of the following scene the rest of the congregants exit.)

CLYDE

That minister sure can talk.
I couldn't get away.

(Sondra, throughout this scene, is coquettish. She is enthusiastic and filled with youthful exuberance.)

SONDRA

Oh, Clyde, I have such good news.
Mother and Father were so impressed with you.
They asked me if I thought
you might come and dine with us next week.
Father said, "What a nice young man,
so hard working and polite."
Mother was dazzled. She said,
"That Clyde's so handsome!"
My sweet Clyde, it's all working out,
just like I told you.

(They kiss. Clyde tries to kiss her again.)

SONDRA

Oh, Clyde, it's Sunday afternoon—not Saturday night.
(Clyde appears quite anxious.)
 Are you all right?

CLYDE

Don't worry. I'm just fine.

SONDRA

So what shall we do next week?

CLYDE

It's just that I'll be busy at the factory
the next few days.
I'll just need a few days to get things done.

SONDRA

    Well, don't take too long.
    Sondra needs to see her sweet Clyde.
    All I want is to be with you.

CLYDE

    It will not take too long.
    All I want is to be with you.

(Sondra kisses him and exits. Clyde walks in the other direction out of the church area and ponders his situation.)

(Finally he begins.)

CLYDE

    It will not take too long.
    I'll need some time to get things done.
    What am I thinking?
    What I've been thinking all these weeks.
    If she would only go away.
    If she'd just leave me here alone.
    It's all so close.
    Everything I want
    I tasted on Sondra's lips.

    The devil's whisper. I hear it now.
    Death!
    Murder!
    The murder of Roberta!
    Someone takes her away.
    Someone—
    Someone else.
    Another man, in another coat, wearing another hat—
    Another man who no one knows.
    Another man who none can trace.

    The devil's whisper!
    In a moment it would end,
    A stone thrown in a stream,
    an unremembered dream.

(Roberta completes packing her suitcase and starts to walk, to begin her journey to join Clyde. When Clyde completes his soliloquy the set transforms into the scene at the lake.)

Another coat. Another hat.
I'd be that man—not me.
Someone else—
Someone who exists just for a day—
Someone with no past who can end all this sorrow.
Someone who will disappear with her tomorrow.

SCENE THREE

(Clyde and Roberta have been having a picnic along the banks of Big Moose Lake. To orchestral accompaniment, we first see Roberta posing for a photograph. After Clyde takes a few pictures, Roberta takes the camera and takes a picture of Clyde. They leave some things on the shore, get into a skiff, and push off into the lake.)

ROBERTA

Isn't it still and peaceful?
It seems to be so restful here.
These trees are so tall.
A fortress protecting
all these fragile water lilies.
All the way through the forest
the road was rough and cool and silent.
And to think it led to a stone church
on the banks of the lake.
A glorious surprise—
Is that where we are to be married?

CLYDE

That's it, Bertie … first thing in the morning.

ROBERTA

When you signed in as Clifford Golden,
I didn't know what to think.

CLYDE

We're not married yet. It wouldn't be right.

ROBERTA

Sure … Of course …Sure.
Clyde, when you marry me
you will see that things can be
just like the way they were.
Remember you told me you loved me?

(Clyde stops paddling. He holds the paddle and thinks about whether to use it to knock Roberta off the side of the boat. Roberta is in a vulnerable position. She is leaning over the bow of the boat, looking first at the water lilies and then at the birds circling above. Ultimately, Clyde cannot bring himself to push Roberta and he puts the paddle down. He picks up the camera to occupy his nervous, slightly shaking hands. He feels defeated.)

ROBERTA

Look, the birds are circling above,
saying goodbye before they go south.

CLYDE

*(Quietly)*I cannot do it.
I cannot do it.

(Clyde looks as if he is going to fall forward into the boat. Roberta turns around and sees him. She is concerned and moves towards him.)

ROBERTA

Clyde! Clyde!
What is it?
Whatever is the matter?
You look so strange. So ... so ...
Why, I never saw you look like this before.
What is it?

(She moves to comfort him.)

CLYDE

No! No! Stay away.
Roberta, stay away!

(She reaches to embrace him.)

ROBERTA

Clyde, dear Clyde!

(Attempting to keep Roberta from embracing him, Clyde swings his arms around wildly. In his hand he is clutching the camera and inadvertently hits Roberta in the face. She is stunned, loses her balance and falls over the side of the boat.)

ROBERTA

Help! Help!
Clyde! Clyde!

(Clyde watches Roberta go down. He is able to save her, but chooses not to. The lights fade.)

SCENE FOUR

(The next Saturday. The Griffiths' vacation home. Samuel is reading on a lounge chair. Clyde enters.)

SAMUEL

Gilbert and Bella will soon be home.
How they love shopping in that motor car!
Don't look so worried, Clyde.
Sondra Finchley's with your cousins.
She'll be back soon.
She's quite a catch.
I'm proud of you, Clyde.
You have earned this chance.

There is something you should know
about our family, son.
When your grandfather died
he left a will….

(Mason enters.)

SAMUEL

Orville! You're a long way from Lycurgus.
I already gave you plenty for your campaign.
Clyde, meet our District Attorney
and next congressman, Mister Orville Mason.

MASON

Sam, I need to talk to your nephew–alone.
Just give me a moment with the boy.

SAMUEL

All right, Orville.
I'll be inside if you need me.

(Samuel exits.)

MASON

You are familiar with Big Moose Lake?

CLYDE

Not really, sir.

MASON

A factory girl, Roberta Alden, was found drowned.
You knew her pretty well.

CLYDE

> Not any better than the other girls.

MASON

> Now really boy, don't waste my time.
> Don't waste my time.
> You deny knowing her?
> You deny that you and she were to be married?
> We have your trunk with Miss Alden's letters.
> I did not march in here with the sheriff
> to save your uncle the shame.
> The sheriff's outside.
> Look, Griffiths, don't deny it.
> Come clean.
> If you have a story to tell,
> start telling it now.
> Now really, boy, don't waste my time.

CLYDE

> But I've done nothing wrong.

(Offstage—or in the orchestration—we hear the honking of Gilbert's car.)

MASON

> *(He notices how nervous Clyde has become.)*
> Let's go explain matters to your family.

CLYDE

> Oh, please, no!

MASON

> Don't want to go?

CLYDE

> I knew her. Of course I did.
> Sure those letters show that.
> But what of it?
> I did not kill her.
> I did not go there to kill her—
> and I didn't, either …
> It was an accident!
> An accident!

(Mason leads Clyde to the sheriff, who comes on and takes Clyde away. Mason starts to return to the house to tell Samuel what has happened, as the set transforms into the Griffiths' home in Lycurgus.)

SCENE FIVE

(At the Griffiths' home.)

ELIZABETH

Accused of murder! Accused of murder!
Oh, Sondra!
How could you be so foolish?
I told Samuel that boy was a mistake.
I told him!
And now that poor girl's letters in the papers!
The story is everywhere!
All people talk about.
Foolish Sondra, so foolish!

SONDRA

Maybe what he says is true.
Maybe it was an accident.

ELIZABETH

Your father's going mad.
He says you might have to move.
Your reputation is ruined!

BELLA

It will not come to that.
Don't worry, Sondra.

GILBERT

Father is bankrolling Mason's run for Congress.

BELLA

He will take care of things.
I'm sure of it.

GILBERT

Keep your name out of it.
I am sure of it.

SONDRA

But maybe what he says is true.

GILBERT

Sondra, you still don't get it.

BELLA

What would that change for you?

GILBERT

What would that change for your family or mine?

(While the following quartet is sung, the chorus gradually appears. They are reading Roberta's letters from the newspapers which have been published during the trial. The chorus members appear on various levels and in different places on the set.)

BELLA

Forget him. Forget him.
He never even existed.
Be seen at the best parties.
You have nothing to hide.

GILBERT AND ELIZABETH

Forget him. Forget him.
Go out with your friends.
Take drives in the motor car.
You have nothing to hide.

SONDRA

(Aside) Forget this, forget him?
Can I forget him?

CHORUS

(Reading Roberta's letters from the newspapers)
My Dearest Clyde, Today I pretended you were coming for me.
And so I bid goodbye to all of my favorite places.
Dear Clyde, I beg you not to torture me.
I trusted you and came home as you asked.
You promised solemnly before I left you would come
for me in three weeks at most.
Solemnly you gave me your word.
Dearest Clyde, today I pretended you were coming for me.
And so I bid goodbye to my favorite places.
Don't make me wait here any more.
Forgive me all the trouble, all the trouble I've caused.
But try and understand how hard it has been for me here.
Don't make me wait here anymore.
Your sorrowful, Roberta.

(The quartet/chorus is suddenly interrupted by the appearance of Elvira. Samuel enters and does not see Elvira. He is carrying the morning paper.)

SAMUEL

    That poor girl's letters were in the paper this morning.
    Mason read them in court.

(Samuel, reading from the newspaper)
    "Please come for me. I've waited for so long."

ELVIRA

    May I have a word with you—
    in private?

SAMUEL

    Certainly.

(Elizabeth, Sondra and Gilbert exit.)

ELVIRA

    I believe my son.
    He says it was an accident.
    Samuel, I want ask you …

SAMUEL

    I felt obliged to see him through the trial
    but will not pay a murderer's appeal.

ELVIRA

    I have not come for money.
    I have not come for *your* money.
    I have come to ask you to come to the courthouse.
    Come to the courthouse.
    Your presence would say
    more than your money.
    You have stayed away.
    For two weeks you've stayed away.
    Clyde will take the stand tomorrow,
    tell the truth tomorrow.
    Come to the courthouse.
    Show that you have faith in Clyde.

SAMUEL

    Have faith? Have faith?
    Believe what you must.
    The defense begins today.

ELVIRA

> For myself I never would have come,
> But for Clyde the sin of pride has fled.
> I fear for my child.
> In my dreams I saw him dead.
> I beg you. I beg you!
> You are the most respected man in town.
> From nothing you built a strong, thriving business.
> Will you not help me save my son?

SAMUEL

> You think that would matter?
> I have done enough.
> I have paid for his defense.
> Don't ask me to do more.

CHORUS

> "The summer will soon be over.
> I am waiting to hear from you.
> You must come for me, take me away.
> I cannot wait forever.
> I know I shall never see any of them again.
> Great heavens, how I do love Mama.
> What shall I do without her?
> Please come. Please come and don't let me wait here."

ELVIRA

> What matters is not what the world says,
> but what Christ says.
> You live in commerce while I live in Christ.
> When I was very young the Lord in His great mercy
> pardoned my sins and showed me His love.
> What could I do but follow Him?
> He helped me when I had nothing.
> Asa and I turned to Christ when we had nothing.
> And He has sustained us.

SAMUEL

> I have done all I can, Elvira.
> I have done all I can.

ELVIRA

> I will pray for you, Samuel.
> God bless you.

SCENE SIX

(Clyde is in a jail cell.)

ELVIRA

> When your uncle brought you here,
> I was afraid.

CLYDE

> I'm sorry, Mama.
> I did nothing wrong.

ELVIRA

> He should be here by you.
> He's stayed away.
> The whole trial, he has stayed away.

CLYDE

> All those reporters.

ELVIRA

> Like locusts.

CLYDE

> I did nothing wrong.

ELVIRA

> You did nothing to deserve this.
> An accident. An accident.
> They will understand. You'll make them understand.
> "By terrible things in righteousness
> wilt thou answer us. O God."
> On the train from Denver,
> as we traveled from the mountains onto the great plains,
> I remembered how Moses came down with God's word
> to a world that had closed its eyes to faith.
> But faith was reborn in Bethlehem
> and every cross we now bear
> is a cross we carry on the road to salvation.
> "By terrible things in righteousness
> wilt thou answer us. O God."
> I don't know why they tell these lies about you.
> For two weeks we've listened to their deceit.
> But your chance begins tomorrow.
> Carry your cross.

ELVIRA (CON'T.)

When you get on the stand—tell the truth,
tell them your heart changed
and you returned to Christ.
You must tell them your heart, inspired by God's love,
let you see the light.
"By terrible things in righteousness
wilt thou answer us. O God."
You are my boy again.
Tell them the truth, my son.
Carry your cross.

(Clyde's jail cell disappears as the set is transformed seamlessly into the courtroom. During the transition Clyde takes the stand.)

SCENE SEVEN

(The courtroom is filled to capacity. Elvira is seated next to Reverend McMillan and some people from a local mission. There are a number of reporters, photographers and spectators crowded into the courtroom. Clyde is on the stand as the scene begins. We join the trial in media res.)

MASON

You said you were drifting together.
The company rule kept you from taking her out,
so you spent your time alone.

CLYDE

Sometimes I thought if I made more money,
if she worked somewhere else,
we could start being open.
Sometimes I thought of marrying her.

MASON

Did you tell her that?

CLYDE

No.

MASON

So when she wrote: *(He reads from his notes)*
"I feel as though you are not coming.
Do you feel nothing at all?
You have promised to marry me."
Are you telling the jury
she was lying, this good, religious girl was lying?

CLYDE

>That was her plan, not mine.
>She wanted to get married.
>The lake ... the inn ...
>It was all her idea.

MASON

>Yes, the inn—
>You registered under Clifford Golden?

CLYDE

>We were not married.
>*She* found brochures at the Utica Station.
>I went there to tell her I could not marry her
>because ...

MASON

>Because of ... Miss X.
>You met another woman and slowly you stopped
>caring for Roberta ... you became ... what was it?
>*(He looks through his notes)* ... "Hypnotized."

CLYDE

>She was very beautiful—much more than Roberta.
>She was different from anyone I'd ever met.
>More independent.
>Everyone paid so much attention to what she did and said.
>She seemed to know more than anyone I ever knew.
>She traveled places, dressed awfully well,
>was very rich and in society.
>And her picture was always in the paper.
>It was all like a dream.
>At first I could not believe she liked me.
>But she did.
>She knew I was poor,
>but she told me she loved me.
>
>I didn't do anything wrong.
>I just did not want Roberta anymore.

MASON

>You—"did not want her anymore."
>How could you tell her you loved her?
>How could you continue to share her bed?

CLYDE

I wanted to tell her,
but I couldn't.

MASON

Or wouldn't.
Weren't you lying to her?
Weren't you lying to Miss X?
Aren't you lying now when you say
that on the boat you had "a change of heart"?

CLYDE

That's what happened.

(The boat is placed in the center of the courtroom.)

MASON

Tell us—tell us, Mr. Griffiths.
You were in the stern and Roberta was in the bow.
You held this camera we fished out of the lake in your hands.

CLYDE

No, Roberta had the camera.
I can show you.

(Clyde gets off the witness stand and walks toward the boat.)

CLYDE

I sat here.

(He gets in the boat.)

CLYDE

I paddled toward some water lilies.
She wanted to see water lilies.

MASON

Had you had your "change of heart"?
Did you tell her you would marry her?

CLYDE

I was not sure ... not sure ...
I paddled toward the water lilies,
looked at the birds circling above,
and when I looked down ...

I told her that we would marry.
She was very happy and moved towards me.
I told her: "Stay low. Stay low."
But she did not listen.
As she stepped towards me she slipped.
The boat went over.
I swam around and looked for her.
Frantically, I looked for her.
I looked!
I could not find her.
But she did not reply.
"Roberta! Roberta! Roberta!
Come on, answer me!"
It was getting dark.
The current was pulling me.
She was lost. I knew she was lost.
I swam to shore to save myself.
I tried. I was confused.

MASON

*(He starts calmly)*You were confused.
You said *she* got brochures in Utica.
Brochures about lakes in the mountains.
Is this one of the brochures?

CLYDE

Yes.

MASON

What does it say on the back?

(Clyde reads it and is stunned, speechless. Mason takes it from him and reads it out loud to the jury.)

"Courtesy of the Ash Inn, Lycurgus, NY."!

MASON

How do you explain that?

(Clyde remains silent.)

MASON

You picked up that brochure in Lycurgus
when you plotted to kill that poor girl.
This story of "a change of heart" is a lie.
Why else would you not use your name at the inn?
Why else would you throw the camera into the lake?
You were Clifford Golden.
If anyone ever found the body,
they'd look for Clifford Golden.
In that poor girl's pocket there was a letter to her mother.
Do you know what she wrote?
That you and she were to be married.
It's all here!

(Holding up the letter, the brochure, the stack of letters to Clyde.)

Proof that you knew this girl.
Proof that you courted her.
Proof you seduced her.
Proof that she was pregnant by you.
And in the face of all of this,
you sit there and tell this jury that your heart changed
and made you stop in your tracks
like Paul on the road to Damascus.

(Elvira can't stand listening to Mason and conspicuously gets up out of her seat and walks to the back of the courtroom.)

Well, Clyde Griffiths,
you can't change a heart you can't find!
A heart buried under so many lies!
You killed a woman; you killed your unborn child.
Your heart was buried under too many lies to change.
Your heart is buried under too many lies to pity.

CLYDE

I ... I ... I told you. I told you how it happened.
I'm sorry. I'm sorry.
But it was all a mistake.
All a mistake!

MASON

She did not slip off that boat.
You pushed her. You pushed her.
With this oar!
Isn't that right?

CHORUS

(The spectators in the courtroom)

> He hit her. She did not slip.
> He hit her. He hit her with that oar.
> He hit that poor girl.
>
> The poor girl. The poor girl.
> He hit her. He hit her.
> She did not slip.
> She did not slip off that boat.
> He killed her. Justice! Justice!

(Mason launches into his summation to the jury.)

MASON

> My friends, I do believe in justice.
> The jury must recognize the concealment of the truth.
> An innocent is dead.
> If we declare life sacred,
> if truth is our standard,
> then you have no recourse.
> Justice. Justice must be done.

(During a histrionic display in which Mason is congratulated on a job well done, Elvira prays.)

ELVIRA

> My son, I do believe my son.
> A mother can recognize
> when her child speaks the truth.
> An accident occurred.
> If we declare life sacred,
> if mercy's our standard,
> then we have no recourse.
> Dear Lord, acquit my son.

(While the jury deliberates, the angry chorus of spectators reviews Mason's case against Clyde.)

CHORUS

> A liar! He killed her.
> He planned it. He planned every detail.
> He registered under Clifford Golden.
> Clifford Golden!
> He picked up that brochure.
> He plotted to kill her. That poor girl.

62

CHORUS (CON'T.)
>Too many lies. So many lies. All lies.
He took her to that lake to kill her.
He killed his unborn child.
He killed her.

JURY
>Guilty as charged.

SCENE EIGHT

(Clyde's jail cell. He is lying on his iron cot. It is the morning of his execution. He opens a bible and takes out a letter. Sondra enters the cell and sings what she has written to Clyde. Clyde imagines that Sondra has come to say goodbye.)

SONDRA
>Clyde, this letter is so that you will not think
that someone once dear to you
has utterly forgotten you.
She has suffered too.
And although she can never understand
how you could have done as you did,
still, even now, although she is never to see you again,
she is not without sorrow and sympathy
and wishes you freedom and happiness.

(Sondra exits the cell. The lights fade on her as she joins Bella and Gilbert. They exit.)

CLYDE
>"Freedom and happiness."
No signature. Nothing.
"Freedom and happiness."
Where are you now, Sondra?
Who are you with?

(Clyde takes the gold lighter out of his pocket and burns the letter from Sondra. On the second level of the set, a panel opens revealing the electric chair. Far upstage, very dimly lit, we see other prisoners in their cells.)

(Elvira enters.)

ELVIRA
>It's almost time, Clyde.
If there's anything you want to confess,
you must confess it now.

(Clyde softly sings to his mother, in order to make sure that no one overhears his comments.)

CLYDE

Mother, it was an accident.
I did not want her to die.
But I did not save her.
I could have saved her.
I let Roberta drown.

ELVIRA

In your heart it was murder, then.

(Elvira breaks down crying.)

Open your heart and pray.

CLYDE

I do pray, mother.

(Elvira does not listen to him.)

ELVIRA

And when you do, tell me you see him—
He who shapes this world.
Clyde, the mercy of God is equal to every sin.

CLYDE

Lord Jesus give me peace.
Lord Jesus give me light.
Lord Jesus give me strength to resist evil thoughts.
Make me worthy in your sight.
I plotted evil. I confess.
But must I die now?
Is there no help for me?
Will you not help me, Lord?

ELVIRA

Wise and righteous are His ways,
His eternal glory let us praise.

(Prison officials enter and begin to prepare Clyde for the electric chair. The lights come up on the other side of the stage on young Clyde. He is in the mission church. He reaches into his pocket and takes out the lighter and begins lighting candles.)

CLYDE

Lead me, lead me, Lord,
and make me righteous.
Oh Lord, deliver me from sin.
Have mercy on me.

ELVIRA

Oh God, forgive my son.

CLYDE

It's all right, Mama.

(Clyde walks out of the cell and slowly walks up the stairs to the electric chair. Elvira and the prison officials follow Clyde. The chorus of prisoners hums soulfully in the background as Clyde walks up the stairs to the electric chair on the second level. As Clyde gets to the top of the stairs, the lights fade on the chorus. Clyde sings with Young Clyde as he approaches the electric chair.)

YOUNG CLYDE

O how sweet to trust in Jesus,
O to trust his cleansing blood;
and in simple faith to plunge me
'neath the healing, cleansing flood!

CLYDE

Lord Jesus give me peace.
Lord Jesus give me light.
Lord Jesus give me strength to go into the dark.
Oh God, oh God release me.

(Clyde reaches the electric chair. The lights fade on all but Young Clyde.)

YOUNG CLYDE

I'm so glad I learned to trust thee,
precious Jesus, Savior, friend;
and I know that thou art with me,
wilt be with me to the end.

(Young Clyde, who has completed lighting the candles, sits down and lights his gold lighter over and over again, and daydreams about all that lies ahead.)

CURTAIN